THIEVES *of* INTIMACY

BY PAULETTE PIERCE HOLLOWAY

Copyright © 2014 by Paulette Pierce Holloway

Thieves Of Intimacy
by Paulette Pierce Holloway

Printed in the United States of America

ISBN 9781498405379

All rights reserved solely by the author. The author guarantees all contents are original and do not infringe upon the legal rights of any other person or work. No part of this book may be reproduced in any form without the permission of the author. The views expressed in this book are not necessarily those of the publisher.

Scripture quotations taken from the King James Version (KJV) – *public domain*

www.xulonpress.com

TABLE OF CONTENTS

Acknowledgements vii
Introduction: Limitations And Challenges ix

Chapter 1:   Sin 17
Chapter 2:   Fear 21
Chapter 3:   Doubt 25
Chapter 4:   Unworthiness 31
Chapter 5:   Laziness 35
Chapter 6:   Unforgiveness 39
Chapter 7:   Pride 45
Chapter 8:   Uncontrolled/Undisciplined Thoughts 49
Chapter 9:   Busyness/Being Too Busy 53
Chapter 10:   Worldly Distractions 59
Chapter 11:   Self Deception 63
Chapter 12:   Unbelief 69

Conclusion 71

THIEVES OF INTIMACY

ACKNOWLEDGEMENTS

─────────◆─────────

How do you honestly respond to a mandate from the Father to write a book on Intimacy? Do you know just how vast that topic is? It is pretty synonymous with a quote from the book <u>Hinds Feet On High Places</u> where the character Much Afraid said something was "preposterously absurd". So here I am, embarking on an assignment that borders on the preposterously absurd, when I consider who God is and how much of an honor it is to be able to claim such a word as intimacy in the same sentence with our great God.

I first have to pause as I begin this effort and acknowledge that God still speaks through His prophets, regardless of the form they come in or the circumstances under which you encounter them. I confess that I was in an unlikely place (I mean visiting a church with a friend that I had not planned to attend in another State) and was directly singled out and maybe should say "called out" by a young preacher who had never seen me before and who put my business in the street in public, decreeing that I was to write a book on prayer. I had known for a while that I was to do something on intimacy with God and at the moment I heard the prophetic word, I knew those two things were linked. This was now over three years ago. Despite my dismay, disobedience, and disinclination, here I am.

With all that said, just know as you journey through this book with me, it is with much fear and trembling that I have obeyed this call. I thank my God for considering me for such an awesome task. I also thank my children whose lives first dictated my need to pray and later inspired me to keep my prayer life growing, which has had the most significant impact on my intimate relationship with the Lord. I must include my friends who hang with me, praying with me and for me, my church family that accepts me and respects the Christ in me, and my family who supports me and loves me unconditionally.

Introduction
LIMITATIONS AND CHALLENGES

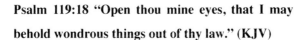

Psalm 119:18 "Open thou mine eyes, that I may behold wondrous things out of thy law." (KJV)

Very early in my faith journey I was drawn to the Word of God. I was allowed the privilege of "having my eyes opened and beholding wondrous things out of God's law". More and more over a period of time, through the wondrous things in God's law, I was drawn into the posture of prayer, recognizing that the most effective prayers were those prayed straight from the Word. A precious sister who has since gone home to be with the Lord, in her message one Saturday morning at an Aglow meeting in Washington, DC said that she sat in prayer with her Bible open to see what the Lord wanted her to pray or to see what He wanted to say to her through the word. That made an amazing impression on me as a baby Christian that day and I found myself trying out the method to see if it held any merit. Thus began my journey into an intimacy that I could never have imagined, not knowing then, that combined, those two spiritual instruments were the most powerful intimacy builders in existence. Through His Word, I discovered that prayer actually changes things, that God is real and that He actually cares and longs for time alone with me. Let me quickly confess that discovery did not come immediately because I had for years beyond measure, only known the God of the universe as Creator and Savior. My formative "religious" years did not afford me the privilege of a broader understanding of God though I am eternally grateful for the introduction that I received. What I came to recognize over a period of time is that as long as you envision God in such a limited way you never move into a place of intimacy because the concept is non-existent. God is way out there in God-land, just watching you and watching out for you, providing and all that, while you live your day to day life. You really "get it" that He has provided eternal life for you through His son, so Savior is not too far-fetched if you can believe. The Creator part as real as that is, had caused me a slight pause, not because of some evolution theory, but because I had read in Isaiah that even the nations are but as a drop in the bucket (Isaiah 40:15), so surely little me must be less than a speck in God's eye. How could God be that carefully interested in such a small speck of His creation? Yet here I am, a living speck that came from somewhere and not like any other speck out there, and clearly not an evolution from any other animal. So though I paused there, I did not park in the long term parking lot. Then there is the undeniable beauty of nature and all that I can see with my eyes, and my matchless love for being one with nature that helped me along as well. I got great help from Matthew 6 when I discovered that he cares about the lilies of the field and the birds in the air. So with that combination of reality I concluded that He must be real and the creator of all things (as you can see, a conclusion drawn almost by default) and just maybe the Creator of the universe actually knows me personally. If you are in any way like me, then it is quite understandable, therefore, for most of us to only reach the Creator and Savior level in our God- journey. And do not misunderstand me; Creator and Savior level is good. It guarantees you an eternity with Him as well as a deep reverence for Him while here in the earth. The news flash is that though you may be limited beyond measure in your introduction to who God is, or perhaps even totally ignorant to who He is, you really can transition to a higher and deeper level with this personal and intimate lover of your soul. I did. I am grateful in saying that the transition, though slow, was sure. The more I read about Him, and shared my heart with Him, the more real He became. The more the lives of the people in the Bible became more than some fairy tale, the more I found myself longing for what I was reading about. When I stumbled upon the passage in the book of James that declared that Elijah was a man like you or me (James 5:12), something seemed to click in my brain and I had one of my first "Aha" moments.

    The fact that God is relational and wants to be in a personal relationship with me was probably my next biggest hurdle. I could finally comprehend that as my Savior He wanted alone-time with me, but to really desire me and find pleasure in my presence was more than I could immediately grasp. I could not imagine this level of intimate, "snuggle up close and stroke my hair" kind of relationship with the Lord God Almighty. The good news is that it did not take the Word long to begin the transition in this area either. As I literally devoured the Old Testament,

I was totally awed by the conversations God had with Abraham, Noah, and Moses. I was further intrigued by His knowing Samuel so well He called him by name and by His reference to David as a man after God's own heart. To me, these were personal intimate conversations, intimate relationships. When God says to you "I am your exceeding great reward" (Genesis 15:1), He is in your face, reassuring you, making promises to you, walking with you, letting you know that you get the absolute best gift of all; you get Him. He's not offering you things or a mate or status or power; He is offering you Himself. It is difficult for even someone like me to diminish the significance of that kind of relationship. Abraham believed God and left his home and family to go to some unknown place just because God said so. He knew that there was something about this God, though he had never seen Him, that he could trust. Most people want that kind of uninhibited trust relationship with perhaps one other human being at best, but to know that kind of relationship with the Living God is mind-blowing.

When God told Noah to build an ark because it was going to rain and Noah had no idea what rain was but trusted the relationship he had with God; that was significant to me (Genesis 6 and 7). Noah had clearly had some experiences with God that made trusting Him through such a preposterous expectation, realistic. God clearly reciprocated the intimate relationship as He described Noah as upright in the midst of such sin and evil. The other side of what made this significant for me is the natural, fleshly side. Noah had to put up with ridicule and harassment from a whole nation of people who laughed at him in his face on a regular basis. Can you imagine? Think about us trying to withstand the pressure of our family and friends calling us a fool and telling us every reason why the one we have chosen to love and to follow anywhere is not the one for us. Instead they are telling us that our choice is beyond foolish; it is dangerous. Many of us would cave under such pressure. Considering how much we long for man's approval, it takes a strong relationship with this "invisible Spirit God" to withstand the pressure of constant human ostracizing.

Then there was Moses, who really took me to another place with the whole relationship concept. Since each of us is different and requires different types of approaches for an effective outcome, God knew Moses would be the one to clinch it for me. Moses' experience at the burning bush was unlike Abraham or Noah because he is the only one of them who knew up front that doing what God said do was like signing his own death warrant. He knew he was a murdering fugitive whose return to Egypt would mean going before Pharaoh for justice (Exodus 2:10-15). Yet, when he encountered the holiness and awesome power of the Living God, he chose to obey and be in relationship with his God even if his very life might be at stake. And the fact that he was somewhat resistant to the plan at first made him all the more like my kind of guy. The kind of sacrifice that Moses made impresses me so because it seems to actually oppose what Satan thinks he knows about us humans when he was taunting God in Job where it says in verse 4 "Skin for Skin! A man will give all he has for his own life". Moses walked into that assignment with eyes wide open defying that concept that a man will give all he has for his life. It is a little more impressive to me to trust someone when you know up front it could cost you your life. For me, that's intimacy personified.

Though I was convinced after considering Moses, I believe the reason I was so intrigued by God's relationship with Samuel was because of my years of working in the field of adoption. Not only was Samuel a toddler whose mother had basically voluntarily placed him in foster care with Eli as the foster parent (I Samuel 1), he was actually adopted by God Himself. When God called him by his name to get his attention, he was outside of the established priestly lineage and except for the vow of a desperate mother had no real likely connection to the priesthood. He was a replacement for who God had positioned to be used (Eli's sons). God seemed to have hand- picked Samuel, trained him, talked to him personally, rebuked him when he leaned to his own understanding (I Samuel 16:1) and gave him step by step instructions on how to get the things done that God wanted done. God was as real to Samuel as any flesh and blood father could have been. I could not compare any earthly father's relationship to the one Samuel had with God and find any area where Samuel lacked anything.

And yes, I mentioned David, the man after God's own heart. I saw myself in David, believing that if David could be that precious to God, after adultery and murder, that even with my sin history, I had a good chance of finding a special place in the heart of such a forgiving and loving God. David even said that God had picked him above all his father's sons, saying God "liked" him (I Chronicles 28:4-KJV) and made him king. I found great comfort in knowing that God loved David intimately and chose him despite his human flaws and I was deeply moved by David's confessions of love for God in the many Psalms he wrote. There was a constant "flavor" of intimacy seasoned throughout.

With all this said, hopefully you are beginning to get a picture of how unlikely I believe myself to be to continue this great assignment, but also that you can relate to my state well enough to keep reading. I am earnestly and honestly moving forward with the expectation that we will both discover more than we ever imagined about the heart of the Father and how He longs for intimacy with us, and that no other relationship can match or surpass such affection.

These chapters are included not to outline a step by step foot guide to intimacy with God, but rather to get your spirit man awakened and help you begin your own personal journey and as necessary, identify and hopefully eliminate, the barriers and limitations, the "thieves", if you will, that may have plagued you in your pursuit of intimacy with God through prayer.

As we begin this journey, I want to take the liberty of defining intimacy just to lay the groundwork. The freeonlinedictionary.com gave six definitions of intimacy and I chose four of them to capture as broad a picture as possible. They are: 1.) a close, familiar, and affectionate personal relationship. 2.) a close association with or deep understanding of a place, subject, etc. 3.) an act or expression serving as a token of familiarity or affection, such as the intimacy of using first names. 4.) privacy, especially as suitable to the telling of a secret. I envisioned all of these in some way as being aspects of intimacy with God.

Chapter One

SIN

Psalm 66:18 "If I regard iniquity in my heart, the Lord will not hear me." (KJV)

I guess the first thing we may need to address now that I have exposed my own limitations, is how to help you identify what the limitations and challenges may be that hinder you from a long desired place of intimacy with your God. The list could be exhaustive and could begin anywhere, but let's begin with the enemy (thief) called <u>sin</u> for the sake of getting started.

The Bible defines sin as all unrighteousness. The Free Online Dictionary defines unrighteousness as failure to adhere to moral principles. It defines sin as a transgression of a religious or moral law, especially when deliberate. Regardless of which definition we choose, the case can be made for the detriment of having sin come between us and our God.

I am not proud to share that there have been some times in my life that my own sin and my inability to release myself from the guilt and weight of it all, literally shut me down, forcing me into a place of isolation from my God. Clearly you must know that He never changed or moved or stopped loving me, but as David confessed in Psalm 51:3b, "My sin is ever before me", so I was the reason for the isolation, not God. I can remember feeling so alone and burdened. Shame even had its place in the emotional baggage I was preparing for the trip I was taking. It was some time later, after way too much wasted "relationship time", that I realized I was far too miserable to be without my God and that I would just have to throw myself at His feet and beg for His forgiveness and mercy. The sad thing about this story is that sin had blinded me to the truth that once I had truly repented, I was forgiven and that according to I John 1 had been cleansed of all unrighteousness. Thus the sin itself not only separates you from your intimate relationship, but the residue of the sin can have long-lasting effects if you allow condemnation to set in.

Many of us are very familiar with the scripture that declares that Satan comes to steal and to kill, and to destroy, even if we don't know exactly where it is found (John 10:10). We quote it and wear it on our sleeves, but we seem not to be able to apply it when we sin. It is as if it does not occur to us that the enemy has come in to destroy our intimacy with the Father by using the lusts of our own flesh to entrap us. Depending on our level of spiritual maturity, the enemy slips in and plants a seed, or he boldly bombards his way in and blatantly sets us up. Either way, sin happens, and we find ourselves in a broken relationship state. As with Eve in the garden, it might begin with a seed questioning what God has said or maybe even questioning God's authority. The act of sin that blossomed from that seed destroyed the intimate relationship man had with God and robbed man of his peace and protection. Or it could be a far more blatant act of sin like King Saul when God specifically told him to destroy all the Amalekites and all their livestock. Saul indeed destroyed the Amalekites, but he decided to spare the best of the livestock, then when confronted by God's prophet, he lied and said the people made him do it and that he only did it to offer a nice sacrifice to God. What he did not know is that sinful act of disobedience would rob him of his throne and snatch it out of the hands of his sons forever (I Samuel 15:3-28).

The unfortunate thing about the way sin works is that once it is conceived, if not quickly confessed, it becomes compounded. The slippery slope of demise begins and we start adding one more thing to one more thing. Whether the sin is stealing, sexual immorality, pride, strife or plain old meanness, if not confessed and dealt with by the power of the Holy Spirit, then the flood gates are opened wide for lying, deceit, manipulation, treachery and even murder to come in. God so desperately wants to protect us from the damage that sin brings and He makes every provision for us not to fall prey to its clutches, yet we find ourselves daily fighting a battle with sin that we often lose.

The scripture in Psalm 66:18 says that if we regard iniquity in our heart, the Lord can't hear us. There is no relationship that exists when one party cannot hear the other. No communication or communion can take place. Sin clearly is the greatest barrier to building intimacy with God and must be dealt with quickly. Once we confess the sin we then must be willing to discipline our lives to protect ourselves from "the sin that so easily besets us" (Hebrews 12:1). Discipline involves daily prayer, study, meditation, denying self and includes fellowship with other like-minded believers. The Holy Spirit will always do His job of leading us and guiding us into all truth (John 16:13), but we have to willingly do our part and submit to Him and not resist Him. We seem to get the anecdote confused when it comes to combatting sin. God says in James 4:7 "Submit yourselves therefore to God. Resist the devil and he will flee from you". Rather what we seem to do is resist God and watch ourselves flee from Him. It is almost as if we desire the fulfilling of the lusts of our flesh far more than we do building an intimate relationship with God. If we truly desire the intimacy with God that we say we do, then we must daily conquer the battle over sin, confessing and repenting when we fall, then quickly getting back up again and running back to the Father who loves us and who is waiting to receive us in His protective care.

Chapter Two

FEAR

---

2 Timothy 1:7 **"For God hath not given us the spirit of fear; but of power, and of love, and of a sound mind." (KJV)**

As I have thought long and hard about the basis and meaning of fear, I confess that it took me some time to come to that "Aha" moment on the issue. The online Webster's definition of fear is "an unpleasant often strong emotion caused by anticipation or awareness of danger". Another internet definition from Wikipedia is "an emotion induced by a perceived threat which causes entities to quickly pull far away from it and usually hide". Both definitions clearly indicate that fear is an emotion and is solely based on the perception of the one experiencing it. Considering the definitions forced me to examine the emotions generated by our perception of danger or discomfort and I was appalled by what I concluded. After I peeled back all the onion layers of rationalization and stood faced with the truth, it occurred to me that the sole basis of fear is that we do not trust God to take care of us in a certain situation. Whatever the dragon is before us, whether a phobia, a real enemy, or an emotionally hurtful situation, we decide that our God is not trustworthy enough to take care of us in that instance. That may seem way over-simplified, but I challenge you to prove this theory wrong.

Once when I was selling Amway products, my "up-line" used a flip chart and marker to help "make the pitch" for us to overcome self-imposed barriers and become sellers in the business, by writing the letters F-E-A-R in a descending straight line on the chart. He then went to each letter and wrote a word for each corresponding letter. Somehow though more than 35 years ago, that visual lesson has stuck with me and I can still chant fear is "False Evidence that Appears Real". He made the point that we stop short of completing some important task because we perceive some obstacle before us to be real. So with that in mind, think about your greatest fear(s) in getting closer to God. Whatever it is, it was created by false evidence. If you fear that you will fail him or you can't be consistent, remember that you are not doing the work in your own strength. If you fear that you will be ridiculed and left isolated, remember that your reputation is safe with him and that he has already promised never to leave you or forsake you. If you fear that you are not good enough to be in his presence, remember that Jesus has paid the price for you, calls you His treasure, and has put you in good and right standing with the Father. If you fear that God is not real and you may be jumping out on a sawed-off limb, just look around at all creation and remember that no human being could have done all this, including create you.

Many years ago, I was given an assignment by the Holy Spirit to give a word of correction/rebuke to a very well-known figure who would be visiting our church. Clearly when I first heard the assignment I did everything I knew to do to discount the voice of the Lord in my ear. I was terrified and then I went on a crash course to prove that God does not do things this way and even if He did, He certainly would not send me to do anything so monumental. I didn't know the man personally; he had no clue who I was except a regular face in a sea of faces. I talked about it with a few friends that I trust with spiritual matters and got fussed at for being a chicken, and even threatened to be exposed to, I guess, the Kingdom Police or somebody. The opportunity to be obedient finally presented itself and I made a couple of feeble attempts to approach the person and chickened out. Finally it was too late and the door was closed. The night that I had the opportunity door slammed in my face, I had a dream. I was in the airport and the person was about to board his plane. I was trying to get to him. I was running through the airport with all my might, hyperventilating, racing toward that gate, jumping over rows of chairs. As I approached the gate, the door closed. I missed it and I woke up covered with perspiration, my heart pounding. I cried in repentance for hours. Fear had not only crippled me, but made me feel worthless, like a big disappointment to God. But God's mercy is everlasting and believe it or not, the next year, around the same time, God spoke the same words and gave me another opportunity to obey. With fear and trembling still my greatest companions, I watched for my "moment", seized it and blurted out what I was told to say like some idiot. I was terrified, knowing that he was going to call me out and turn me over to the Kingdom Police for having the audacity to approach him, a person who did not know me except from a sea of faces in a public setting. Yes, I did it, but fear was my dominant friend at that moment. The amazing thing about fear is that it is just what it is represented to be, "false" evidence. Once I had awkwardly said what I had said, the person looked at me, smiled and said "That's a good word. I receive that". Can you believe that? He received it. I just stood there motionless, unbelieving, excited, blown away. The man moved on and it was over. I want you to know that the next year (by now I guess you have figured out that it was an annual event) he sought me out of the faces in the crowd to shake my hand and to demonstrate that what I had heard was from God and that I had done what God said do. For a "chicken little" God's grace doesn't get any better than that. At that very moment I could not imagine anything more precious to me than being in an intimate personal relationship with such a merciful and gracious God, even when I am not behaving as though I have power, love or a sound mind.

On a recent occasion, I was watching the previews from an upcoming movie that I am sure has now aired long ago, and the character being played by Will Smith made a statement to his son. He said "Fear is not real. Danger is real; but fear is not real". That stuck with me. I modified the statement to say "Fear is not real. God is real". He is more real than your phobia, your eminent danger or your emotional trauma. As I move on to the next challenge, my prayer is that you, too, will remember that fear is not real unless you make it real; it is not from God, and you never need to allow it to interfere with, undermine or plague your intimacy with the Father any more.

Chapter Three

DOUBT

Acts 10:19-21 "While Peter thought on the vision, the Spirit said unto him, Behold, three men seek thee. Arise therefore, and get thee down, and go with them, doubting nothing: for I have sent them. Then Peter went down to the men which were sent unto him from Cornelius; and said, Behold, I am he whom ye seek: what is the cause wherefore ye are come?" (KJV)

Without any formal ranking or prioritizing of these challenges, let's now consider doubt. The online Webster's definition of doubt is "uncertainty of belief or opinion that often interferes with decision-making". The Wikipedia definition is "a status between belief and disbelief, involves uncertainty or distrust or lack of sureness of an alleged fact, an action, a motive, or a decision". Doubt brings into question some notion of a perceived "reality", and may involve delaying or rejecting relevant action out of concerns for mistakes or faults or appropriateness.

Many people will often use fear and doubt synonymously when expressing themselves, but they are quite different, yet both are equally paralyzing and damaging to building an intimate relationship. They both rob you of the key ingredient to intimacy which is trust. If there is constant doubt about another's motives or sincerity, then it becomes very challenging to relax, to be at peace, to rest in the security of the relationship. Doubt can delay making a meaningful commitment or possibly even sabotage the foundation of the relationship.

Because of how great and awesome God is, we can sometimes doubt that He cares for someone as small and seemingly insignificant as us. We doubt whether He is who He says He is. We doubt that He will do what He says He will do. We doubt His Word. We doubt His love for us. And the doubts just keep on going. The truth of the matter is that we doubt those things that we think are too good to be true. With that in mind, I clearly understand why we would doubt the things of God because He really is so good and so pure and so holy that it is hard to fathom that He would want to be in our presence or more, want us in His.

Doubt is one of those "mind-positions" that becomes our best aide in talking ourselves out of something meaningful or good. We may encounter the person that if we would let our guard down and honestly pursue being in a vulnerable and intimate relationship with them, we would have a spouse or friend for life. Rather what we do instead is look for every reason not to trust them, always searching for their motives and constantly undermining the peace that should come from being in a solid relationship. There are many people simply existing today who "doubted the obvious" and let a "good thing" slip through their fingers.

We have done no less with God, and the numbers may be far more astonishing on the side of failed intimacy with God than with people. One of the greatest challenges for us in building intimacy and overcoming doubt is believing that we know His voice. No matter that He has said in John 10:3-5 that His sheep hear His voice and they will not follow a stranger's, we still agonize over whether it was the Lord that we heard speaking into our spirit. Though God has chosen to use the human experience to help us in our development of intimacy we still seem to struggle. I like to use the analogy of talking on the telephone to make the point. I often say that if I talk to someone on the phone only once or twice and over distant periods of time, I am not likely to remember their voice should they call. On the other hand, if I talk to someone every day I will quickly recognize their voice on the phone and they never have to identify themselves when they call. The point of course, is that if you get into the habit of talking to the Lord often, spending time in prayer, listening for His response, you learn to identify His voice. Even when the information challenges you or gives you assignments you would prefer to pass to someone else or alerts you to expect something that is preposterously absurd, you still know if it is the voice of your Heavenly Father.

There are far too numerous occasions that I have allowed doubt to rob me of a deeper level of intimacy with God, and miss out on some precious gift, opportunity or experience, but I will share one in particular. I was attending a Christian women's conference many years ago and the speaker on the stage at the time was from Israel. He was sharing things about Israel with such passion that I felt this longing in my heart to go to Israel that I had not experienced before. There was a plea made for those who had a desire to travel to Israel to begin right then, believing God to go. I immediately felt a passionate response to the challenge stirring in my heart and knew that I was to believe God to go to Israel. Once the cost for the trip was announced later, I knew that was way out of my financial budget so I began to reexamine what was happening to me, doubting that it could be the Holy Spirit working and deciding that I had been caught up in a moment of emotionalism. Understand that at this time, I was a mature Christian who had learned to trust God in many ways. I had enough experience with Him to know His voice. I recognized His stirrings in my spirit; trusting Him for provision was a regular occurrence for me, and yet once I heard how much the trip would cost I began to doubt if it was God at all. I began rationalizing that it was only my fleshly desire to go to Israel that was kicking in. After that session was over, but before the conference ended, I had the conversation with a few other ladies about making the trip and several of them also expressed a desire to go. They seemed not to have the same financial limitations as I did as a single mother recovering from a divorce, so for them, making the trip was quite feasible. Their enthusiasm only made my desire to go grow stronger, but their enthusiasm did not change my financial picture. I chose to doubt that what I was experiencing was God speaking to my heart and I disappointedly started moving away from Him in my heart. I did not want to be close to Him because I had begun to doubt knowing His voice and then slipped into fear that I might hear something else that was not Him. In just a few moments I had slipped into a quiet lull in the spirit. Earlier in the session, when the details of the trip were being advertised, it had been shared that since this was a group sponsored trip being booked through a special travel agent, there was a special financial opportunity being offered. The announcer specified that if a coordinator could get five people to pay for the trip in full, the sixth person, the coordinator, could go for free. Of course I heard that along with everyone else, but by now you have figured out that I am sometimes not the brightest crayon in the box. I let doubt rule me and I gave up. What I had not considered was that for many years, I had somehow managed to take on the role of trip planner/organizer for the many women who attended the conferences with me, making sure that we had plenty of excitement in whatever new city we visited. The women usually relied on me to identify what sites to visit and when and how we would get to the sites. Do I dare tell you that five such women got together and generously agreed to go to Israel and to make me the coordinator of the trip so that I could go for free? Can you believe that? Other groups of six were making the decision to travel together, but they were making the decision to equally divide the total cost of five people between the entire six people in the group, to lower each person's cost, not have five people pay full price and let one person go for free. God used those precious ladies to bring to pass what He had deposited in my spirit even after I doubted that it was Him speaking to my heart or that if it was Him, it surely could not be possible for this trip. It was only because of my relationship with Him that I was able to receive the incredible provision that He had made, without doubting the purity of the ladies' motives. I was even able to maintain my level of dignity while on the trip, because not one of those women ever brought up how we got there, all this even after doubting the goodness of my God. The experience taught me a valuable lesson about the fallacy of running from God, shutting Him out when I think I have missed Him, doubting that I hear Him, and allowing that doubt to rob me of a sweet and intimate time of fellowship with my God.

Just remember that doubt is designed to paralyze you from making a decision by raising questions and insecurities that rob you of realizing what God has spoken or receiving what He has promised. Intimacy nourished through prayer is the vaccine against such paralysis.

Chapter Four

UNWORTHINESS

Luke 7:6 "Then Jesus went with them. And when he was now not far from the house, the centurion sent friends to him, saying unto him, Lord, trouble not thyself: for I am not worthy that thou shouldest enter under my roof:" (KJV)

There is a vile enemy of intimacy with God that is sometimes not tackled even in prayer. As a matter of fact, the more time spent in prayer the more the person who struggles with poor self-worth can retreat from the presence of God. Webster defines being unworthy as "lacking in excellence or value". The Free Online Dictionary further defines it as "insufficient in worth; undeserving".

The enemy called unworthiness can be so overwhelming and deceitful that the person experiencing such can often begin to slide into a place of feigned humility, especially in prayer. When there is little ability to see ourselves the way God sees us we often approach Him with an attitude of what we define as reverence and godly fear, but in actuality is low self-esteem. We are not like the sinner at the temple who strikes his chest with his head bowed, seeing our own sinful state in the presence of a holy God. We are more like a manipulative deceiver trying to make ourselves sound worshipful and respectful acknowledging that we have no right being in God's presence, but rather hoping it will impress Him with our humble presentation.

Being tricked into the false acceptance of low self-worth is a process rather than an event. Many of us did not get the healthy encouragement and support that God intended for each of His children. Worse than that, many were brutally abused, emotionally scarred, abandoned, rejected, even discarded as trash. Once the enemy saw the opportunities for destruction that may have been fostered by those that should have been trustworthy, he took advantage of every opportunity to whisper into our spirit that our victimization was our own fault. He may have even said we deserved it or still worse, that we liked it. We became comfortable in our misery, defeated in our attitude and easily convinced that we had no value. Once we bought into the lie, Satan did not have to work so hard because we became our worse enemy.

As we accepted Christ as our Savior, going into the presence of God certainly strengthened us because of the very nature of His presence, yet we ourselves remained the barrier between true intimacy and powerful prayer. Our encounters with God were more those of dutiful rituals rather than intimate precious love-filled, awe-filled communion. God remains the same, loving us, keeping us, providing for us, pursuing us, desiring us, while we consciously and unconsciously question Him, wondering why He loves us so much. As we practice walking in our place of devalue, secretly contradicting all that is true, we find it harder to accept God's love, His forgiveness, or that He has a good plan for our lives. We understand in our limited way, that God has good intentions, and we want the benefit of that, but we cannot break through that massive barrier created by our inability to accept our own value. If we consider the lame man at the pool of Bethesda, when Jesus approached him and asked him if he wanted to be made whole, he immediately responded with his pitiful "woe is me" state. (John 5) Here he was in the very presence of the Healer, and he could only relate to his own short comings and unfortunate circumstances. After all, he had been lame for 38 years, and no one had thought enough of him so far to get him into the pool to receive healing. He seemingly had no value to anyone, not even to himself. Sometimes we respond to being in the presence of the Healer in a similar way, reflecting only what we believe about ourselves or what we think others believe about us. God wants us to see ourselves the way He sees us and respond without hesitation to His invitation to be healed and come into His presence.

    I can remember having many challenges growing up, being very sick, having extended periods of hospitalization which resulted in many surgeries that left me feeling ugly and being rejected by those that I wanted to accept and love me. I struggled with my self-worth, married very young and after a while found myself in an abusive relationship. I stayed much longer than I should have, thinking that it was just my cross to bear. Once out of that relationship, I chose another where I was disrespected on several levels, but again accepted things as my cross to bear. I had grown tremendously in my relationship with the Lord during those seasons, but I still found myself stuck in the mire of low self-worth, rationalizing others' behavior, keeping secrets, denying personal emotional pain, and escaping my plight through good works and keeping busy. Because of the incredible faithfulness of God, He nurtured me and wooed me, and poured out His amazing grace on me and began turning around the huge cargo ship of low self-worth. Not only did He reverse the direction of the ship, He literally changed or should I say exchanged the cargo. He introduced me to the truth of Psalm 139:14-17 declaring that I am fearfully and wonderfully made and that His thoughts are precious toward me. He loved me to the place of realizing that He does not make junk, and that I am high up on His list of favorites.

My prayer is that as you read this section, something significant will grab your heart and you will willingly admit that you have thought lies about yourself. Confess them as sin and render those thoughts as powerless over you forever. God is waiting for you to see yourself as He sees you, so that you can sweetly, passionately, and with a blessed assurance enter into His presence where you can be introduced to a level of intimacy unknown to you and surpassed by no other. "Thou wilt shew me the path of life: in thy presence is fulness of joy; at thy right hand there are pleasures for evermore." (Psalm 16:11 KJV)

Chapter Five

LAZINESS

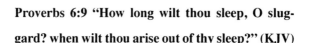

Proverbs 6:9 "How long wilt thou sleep, O sluggard? when wilt thou arise out of thy sleep?" (KJV)

With the discussion of laziness, you may be ready to start your debate with me now, and accuse me of moving from ministry to meddling. None of us likes to think of ourselves as lazy. It does not gain us much respect from others and does nothing for our self-image. Laziness as defined by the Wikipedia is "a disinclination to activity or exertion despite having the ability to do so". The Online Dictionary goes on to say it means "resistant to work or exertion; disposed to idleness". I tend to lean more toward the Wikipedia definition capturing the concept of not doing something though you have the ability to do so. We often fail to develop any meaningful prayer life simply because we do not want to get out of the bed. We succumb to the thoughts in our mind that tell us we are too tired, too sleepy; it's too early or too late.

Of course, another side of the laziness challenge is that you are not in bed, but perhaps you are looking at television or "chillin" on the sofa or doing some other relaxing meaningless thing. You're on Facebook or you're playing a game on your phone or you're just randomly surfing the net. You are not doing anything special and simply don't want to do anything. You might even say you don't feel like doing anything. You just want to relax. Your mind does not wander to prayer; your heart does not long for intimacy; you just want to relax. A small justification might even stir in you that you deserve to rest; with all that you do, you deserve to relax.

Let's talk about this. Let's start our dialogue by comparing intimacy with God to a physical relationship (which we know is truly no comparison). But for the sake of discussion it might be easier to see this if we first approach it from a natural perspective. You have a spouse that you love dearly and you want to see your relationship flourish. Daily you decide to get up before your spouse awakes and quietly go to the gym, making sure you do not disturb his or her sleep. That is so considerate of you, by the way. You return home just as your spouse is heading out the door for work. There is a warm greeting exchanged and a friendly kiss as you pass each other. In the evening, you both return home and go to your separate corners to have some "me" time after a long day. You have dinner in the same room while chatting on the phone or occupying yourselves in some way. At bedtime you climb into your king-sized bed and have a brief conversation about each other's day, grab your favorite reading material and check out for the night. Occasionally, during your week, there is a tender time of intimacy that comes with the dutiful expectations of marriage. By all outside appearances this is a good relationship, but the question arises, "Is it intimate?" Has either partner been willing to sacrifice personal time to communicate feelings, invest time, share experiences, do special things, or just sit and enjoy the other's presence? All of those sacrifices take a deliberate purposeful effort and few of us are willing to make those kinds of sacrifices, especially when things seem to be going well and no one is making waves. As good as that relationship may appear to the average observer, it still does not readily meet the characteristics of intimacy. Consistent, yes. Reliable, yes. Rewarding, maybe. But intimate, not necessarily. Perhaps ritualistic would better describe it. Neither person has demonstrated that they are willing to get up earlier or stay up later, or plan an activity or massage the others' back. It takes more to build intimacy than maintaining a pleasant relationship and sharing the same bed, and so does building an intimate relationship with the Father. Energy has to be expended; investments must be made; time must be dedicated. Sacrifices must be made. You have to study your partner; share and listen. You have to go the extra mile for that special love gift that can only be found in an inconvenient place. You have to stay up late and wait for that plane to land or get up early to get to the airport. You have to clean up that mess or walk the dog. It's work. If you do not invest the work, then the relationship becomes dull. There is no such thing as a strong healthy relationship that is maintained by lazy people. Since God is always there, promising never to leave us, promising that nothing can ever separate us from His love, always working on our behalf, clearly if there is a problem we are the culprit.

I have discovered that if I do not follow the regimen that my dentist has given, daily flossing, twice brushing, added plaque fighters, rituals and more rituals; when I go for my check up, I have plaque build-up, cavities and possibly a threat of a scaling. It is a lot of work, but the benefits far outweigh the constant inconvenience of the sacrifices. Breaking my routine of spending quality time in the morning and at night, and building in any other brief or special times throughout the day to be in God's presence has proven to have far greater benefits than getting a good report at the dentist. Am I often sleepy or tired or busy? Absolutely! But I press during those times for fear of falling into a trap of convenience. I have discovered that convenience and complacency are great teammates of laziness. They support and inspire, making it easy to put off carving out that special time until later. God wants us. He does not care about our things, or our accomplishments or our status; He wants us. When we allow our own laziness to be the thief that robs us, we make a clear statement to our Heavenly Father that we do not want Him; we just want what He can do or what he can give. I do not believe that any of us really want to send God that message. So with that said, "Wake up! Get up! Sing! Pray! Worship! Spend quality time with the lover of your soul."

Chapter Six

UNFORGIVENESS

Matthew 6:14-15 "For if ye forgive men their trespasses, your heavenly Father will also forgive you: [15] But if ye forgive not men their trespasses, neither will your Father forgive your trespasses." (KJV)

How much time do you spend tallying up the score against those who have "done you wrong"? Do you allow offenses to dominate your thoughts? Can you face those who you perceive as perpetrators against you with genuine peace? Do you see yourself as a victim in your personal, spiritual, social or professional relationships? These are all questions that when answered might be able to help you determine if you are harboring unforgiveness against someone. Forgiveness has been defined in a number of ways and I will share a few of them. The Merriam-Webster Online Dictionary defines forgiveness as: "to give up resentment of or claim to requital for; to grant relief from payment of; to cease to feel resentment against." Dictionary. Reference.com defines forgiveness as "to grant pardon for or remission of (an offense, debt, etc.); absolve; to give up all claim on the account of; remit (a debt, obligation, etc); to cease to feel resentment against: to forgive one's enemies; to cancel an indebtedness or liability of." If any of these definitions strike a chord with you, then we need to talk.

Unforgiveness can be another one of those tricky barriers because our rational thinking that we can call our ego, tells us that the perpetrator deserves the treatment or attitude we hold on to. After all, we do have to protect ourselves. Certainly God does not expect us to forget such a hurtful wrong done against us. We would be a fool to keep setting ourselves up and have others judge us for our weaknesses. Can you identify with anything so far? It does not seem to matter that God has put a qualifier on forgiveness saying that He forgives as we forgive. We bypass the qualifier because our situation is different. We are tricked by our own desire for retribution.

Because forgiveness is a spiritual principle it is not something that can be accomplished simply because you will it to be so. There are spiritual components that can only be realized by spiritual means. Love, of course, is the first and foremost of all spiritual attributes which propels everything else that we ascribe to. Paul reminds us in Galatians that even our faith works by love (Galatians 5:6). He emphasizes in I Corinthians 13:5 (The Message) that love does not keep score, and goes on to tell us that love never looks back but keeps going until the end. So clearly if we apply the law of love we can be poised to forgive.

Working in total concert with love is the spiritual attribute of humility. Humility is defined by the online Wikipedia as the act or posture of lowering one-self in relation to others. From a biblical context it may be best defined by Paul as not thinking of yourself more highly than you should (Romans 12:3). If we can get ourselves out of the way, not demand our own rights, and trust God to handle any and all offenses whether perceived or real, then we are getting in position for forgiveness to be manifested. The struggle often comes when we cannot get pass the fact that someone "did us wrong". It takes divine intervention for us to humble ourselves to the point of not wanting to keep score of some wrong done to us. Humility is an attribute granted to us directly from Christ Himself, so to be lacking in humility simply requires more desire to be like Christ, who the word says humbled Himself to give up His status in heaven, take on the form of man, then die the most demeaning and excruciating death imaginable (Philippians 2:3-8). He did all that to give man the only way back to the Father. And He did all that knowing that man would disobey Him, deny Him, disrespect Him, even kill Him. Now that's humility.

There are many testimonies of forgiveness that I can share because I have lived through some very tough situations over the years. Unfortunately, the greatest acts of forgiveness that God has worked in me also come with very personal and specific incidents that I do not believe it is appropriate to disclose in such a public venue. There is one that I can share however, if you will forgive some of its vagueness. Many years ago in my days of "ignorance to the ways of Christ" I was challenged by a person who blatantly did me wrong. This was a person that I trusted and was in good relationship with, at least from where I stood. A very serious situation occurred and it became adversarial, putting my friend in somewhat of a "tie-breaker" position. She knew my character and my history concerning the situation, but out of fear of rejection she made a decision to align herself with the "other side" and things did not go well for me. I was so hurt, then angry, then bitter, then totally disengaged. After a while I simply dismissed the relationship as non-existent and moved on, or at least so I thought. Because God loves me so much and always keeps His end of the deal when I bargain with Him to grow up, opportunities to encounter the person kept presenting themselves and I would find myself having feelings of anger each time. Finally, with a whole lot of God's nudging, I decided that being angry with someone was so unprofitable for me and was causing me to avoid situations where I would otherwise have enjoyed. Fortunately for me, my logic seems to have the ability to outweigh my emotions in many instances, and being angry and missing out on things that I wanted to enjoy seemed illogical to me. I did not know God so well back then, but even then, He had begun a good work in me and I found myself softening to the hurt and to the person. It wasn't very long before I had made a conscious decision to release the debt because carrying around the invoice was just too weighty. I praise God for His faithfulness to me, teaching me His principles, showing me how to apply the "Law of Love" even before I fully understood those principles. I can now tell you that what God has done for me has worked such a miracle in my heart that I find it difficult to hold on to offenses. Even now, as I recall to mind some hurdles I have overcome, I cannot dig up any old wounds, hurt, shame, or blame against others. God's work is so thorough and His rewards are so great, that I find it much easier to lay my burdens on Him quickly so that I can continue to love and bless others. It is such a pleasure to be in His presence, feeling the joy of His love and the comfort of His peace, relishing in the sweet intimacy that comes with knowing He loves me through every offense and heals every wound brought against me. Experiencing that "Aha" moment, that I am not a victim but a victor, is pretty nice too. So let go of unforgiveness and allow the forgiveness that God promises you when you forgive to flow freely in your direction.

Chapter Seven
PRIDE

Psalms 10:4 "The wicked, through the pride of his countenance, will not seek after God: God is not in all his thoughts." (KJV)

When I think of pride, I often think of the arrogant, the haughty, the self-elevated, or even the pushy or controlling. Though all of those synonyms may capture the concept, I want us to expand our discussion to also include some possibly more subtle aspects of pride that could rob of us an intimate relationship with our God. Pride is defined by Miriam Webster's on line dictionary as a feeling that you respect yourself and deserve to be respected by other people: a feeling that you are more important or better than other people: a feeling of happiness that you get when you or someone you know does something good, difficult, etc. The second definition is probably the most familiar to us and certainly comes with its downfalls, especially because God has made it clear that He hates pride and punishes those who walk in it

(Daniel 5:20), but the first and last definitions can also be a snare to us as we cultivate intimacy with God.

Let's talk about what could possibly go wrong merely because you respect yourself and deserve to be respected by others. Surely that is a sound and healthy position so there should not be any danger in taking such a position. What might need to be considered here, is what happens to us when we deserve and rightly expect others to respect us, but they do not. What do you do? Do you demand respect? Do you confront them? Do you walk away wounded? This can be a tough one only because that unsatisfied demand for respect can slip off into a place of unforgiveness, which if examined closely is simply a place of pride. Your pride or your ego alerts you that you have been disrespected and that should not be tolerated because respect is what you deserve. All people deserve to be respected. The truth of the matter is that we are not always going to be given the respect that we deserve and we're not always going to be able to get that rectified, so what is our next step? We have to call on the spiritual virtue of humility and allow God to rescue us from ourselves. Humility is the remedy for pride. Humility allows us to ignite the virtue of grace. Humility gives us the license to move on, to cancel the debt, regardless of what the other person does. Humility draws the attention from us and puts it on Jesus. And once we can get the attention off us we can let go of that sense of entitlement that motivates us to demand retribution. It is only when we are walking in humility that we are able to sit in God's presence, recognizing that nothing that we endure is comparable to what Christ suffered for us. We are then better able to grasp that our Holy Father gave His very best gift to us, to become sin for us, to be beaten and bruised for us, so that we could live the abundant life and spend eternity with our loving Holy Father. That recognition strips away all of our sense of pride and brings us down to the level of awe and longing. We learn to desire God's presence and the intimacy that comes with knowing that He also desires us.

You may now also be wondering how a harmless feeling of happiness that comes when we or someone we know does something good could in any way be a snare to intimacy, and I'm glad you mentioned it. Let's consider the outstanding job you did and the amazing reaction that followed and the satisfaction that settled in your chest from a job well done. It was as simple as that. You felt good! In that moment you basked in the feeling of a good accomplishment and enjoyed the warmth of that place. Because that place is such a pleasant one for us humans, it can also be a bit addictive. We enjoy compliments, accolades, things that bolster our ego. It's how we are wired, so surely God knows that about us. And surely God is not trying to take that little human feature away. So where is the danger? The danger is the sense of "self-satisfaction". Once we enjoy that moment of "self-accomplishment", get that sense of "self-satisfaction", we have to be extremely "God-minded" to shift immediately to the place of praise and glory to God. We surely know that God did it and we testify to that effect at Wednesday night prayer meeting, but truth be told, that was not our initial thought or response. For an instant we felt pretty good about how well we did, how good we are, how good others think we are. Just be careful. As innocently as that personal sense of pride in our accomplishment comes in, we store that feeling and sometimes subconsciously, we do things that will generate that feeling again. It can soon become all about us and the prayer meeting testimony begins to sound a little like bragging to the poor worshippers who have to listen to you. The danger to intimacy with God is that the better you think you are, the less you rely on Him, and He is extremely jealous. He wants our total dependence, so what can appear to be an innocent sense of well-being because of a good accomplishment could be the top of the slippery slope that slides downward to the place of pride and self-reliance. Personally, I have had to have many conversations with self because I am gifted in many ways and often find myself being congratulated for some nice thing "I've" done. I need the Holy Spirit to stay right in my ear to keep me in check and to combat that subtle demon of pride that easily rears its ugly head. I need my God-dependence and I stay alert for those lurking subtleties that might lure me from my intimate secure place with the Father.

Chapter Eight

UNCONTROLLED/ UNDISCIPLINED THOUGHTS

Ezekiel 11:15 "And the Spirit of the Lord fell upon me, and said unto me, Speak; Thus saith the Lord; Thus have ye said, O house of Israel: for I know the things that come into your mind, every one of them." (KJV)

This thief may be the toughest yet to conquer because it is tricky, intrusive, abrupt, and sometimes just plain rude. The thief of undisciplined thoughts has taken many prisoners and has sentenced many to an untimely relationship death. Imagine being in the midst of prayer or meditation, focused and deliberate, and like an unexpected burglar thoughts jump through the window and your concentration is invaded. No more are you totally focused on the love of God and the power of His word, you are now pushing aside the conversation you had yesterday or the answer to the question of whether the oven is off or if today is the day you had that appointment. The person who can master control of his thoughts is well on the way to building a life of intimacy with the Father.

One of the areas of undisciplined thoughts that really seems to take us down an unwanted path is the area that involves our emotions. I have discovered that when I am in an emotional upheaval, despite my best efforts to corral the thoughts that accompany those emotions, I find myself thinking about what has me upset or disappointed or excited. If the emotions are related to a bad experience, then I am more likely to have a greater struggle.

For years, when confronted with an emotional challenge I would find myself stuck in that place of heaviness, feeling like a 200 pound person was sitting inside my chest or pulling down on the back of my neck. No matter how I tried to shake it and move into a quality place of worship, I would have little success. The good news about how I am wired is that (most days) I am a logical analytical type. So what happens to me is that I see myself stuck and weighted down and I tolerate it for a while, and then I start analyzing myself. It does not take me long to get to the place where I cannot find anything profitable in the state I'm in, so I then am able to make a choice. I believe that one of the most impactful "aha moments" I ever had was when I read in I Corinthians 6:12 and again in 10:23 that Paul said "All things were lawful for him, but not all things were expedient". That concept really struck me and I found myself checking out things in my life that may not be expedient or profitable or beneficial. Once I began this routine, it became easy to identify when I was in an emotional place that was not profitable or beneficial.

Granted, it was not always instantly rectified, but identifying it would be a good catalyst to get me thinking and then moving me to making a choice. I began working on solutions to overcome my toxic thoughts. I did not realize back then that I was building an arsenal to combat undisciplined thoughts. I would start by engaging in a deep breathing exercise. I would simply inhale deeply while whispering "In Holy Spirit"; then I would exaggeratedly exhale while saying "Out with the trash". I would do this over and over. I would be so focused on my breathing and reciting that there would be no room for other thoughts. Then I would move into a weak praise (because weak was all I could muster at first), declaring how great God is. What I discovered is that the more I praised, the stronger I got and before very long I would be in a full and powerful praise, sometimes yelling and singing. Then as I grew, I began making up songs by putting some scripture into a song, imagining myself to be like David. Reflecting on those days even now brings fond memories to my heart because I recognize that I still use those same weapons today in some form or the other.

As I am sitting before the Lord in worship and something ugly or disruptive rears its head, I begin singing a worship song. I realize that I cannot hold two opposing thoughts in my head at the same time. I become more deliberate and intense in my listening or meditating or reading and I quickly ask for help from my experienced "Helper" to keep me on track. I remind myself that my place of perfect peace only exists in the mental land where my mind is "stayed on Him" (Isaiah 26:3). Sometimes I begin humming some familiar hymn or composing some thankful lyric. The antidote may vary but the outcome is always the same. The power of the Holy Spirit moves in and I get the help I need to continue in my quest to be in the Lord's presence, while getting the added benefit of having my mind renewed.

One of the encouraging things about pursuing God and desiring to experience His presence is that He is so loving and faithful, and meets you wherever you are on the journey. And because He discerns our very thoughts and intentions of our hearts (Hebrews 4:12), He does not get taken by surprise when the thought pops up. He already knows the righteous intent of our heart and has already seen the thoughts coming and has put in place what is needed to get us back on track. It is right at that point that you can be reminded that God desires intimacy with you and as a matchless lover of your soul, He goes far beyond our limited abilities to build the level of intimacy we both desire. So as you pursue God's presence and fall prey to those merciless unwanted intruders called thoughts, be encouraged that God wants you more than you can imagine and is willing to do whatever it takes to woo you, win you and nurture you forever.

Chapter Nine

BUSYNESS/BEING TOO BUSY

Luke 10:40-41 "But Martha was cumbered about much serving, and came to him, and said, Lord, dost thou not care that my sister hath left me to serve alone? bid her therefore that she help me. 41 Jesus answered and said unto her, Martha, Martha, thou art careful and troubled about many things:" (KJV)

Many of you reading this chapter might now move into your judgmental spirit and say I am now moving into the realm of meddling and detouring off the highway of ministering. After all, James 2:20 is clear that "Faith without works is dead". Further, the Church cannot operate without the "worker bees" that get things done, so where could this chapter possibly take us? Well let's see if there could be any dispute that our being busy even with religious or spiritual matters is not necessarily being good stewards over our time or even embracing the best Gift. If we wanted to use the scripture referenced in this section as a springboard for discussion, we might begin with whether you think Martha was a worshipper, desiring intimacy with the Savior or a worker desiring to show off her gift of hospitality. She clearly had His interest at heart, wanting to make sure His physical needs were met. She clearly had a personal relationship with Him because she was hosting Him in her home and there is no indication that either of them was uncomfortable with that. She clearly knew something about who He was and believed Him to be someone special, at the least, a teacher sent from God because she could observe her sister doing "nothing" but sitting at His feet soaking up every word. Yet, knowing all those things, Martha was busy being "the hostess with the mostess" and failed to savor her time with the Lord; the King of Kings who was finding respite under her very roof. Martha may have been like some of us today; being satisfied to know Him casually, content to know that others know that we know Him, and a bit indignant that those who claim to know Him and love Him do very little to show it.

In this fast paced age that we now live, it is easy to become so busy we don't have time for lengthy personal devotions and Bible reading. Whether or not we work outside the home, we are busy. We have the gym and the vet and the spa and the vacation and shopping and the children and the meeting and so on. I know you get the idea. We awake to a full schedule that must be met and God forbid we oversleep. We immediately start shaving things off the front end so we can get on track for the important things like getting to work on time or catching that train or making that appointment. We might shorten our shower, skip breakfast, do our make-up on the run or wear something that requires no preparation, but our goal is to keep that appointment. If we have a heart for God, but not a lot of time, spending quality time with Him might not make the cut either. Maybe a quickie prayer and a passage from a nice devotional will be enough to ease our conscience when we are on the move. Or maybe a postponement of communication until we are in the car or at our desk might be the order of business. If none of these things are rolling down your street then I applaud you, but if there was a speed bump that slowed you down, you may be entertaining a shrewd thief.

The last paragraph describes only one category of theft and is likely to hit home with all of us at some point. A more dangerous category is when, like Martha, we are busy doing the work of the church, respectable "Kingdom" work that undeniably must be done. We serve in ministries; we are faithful in attendance; we are committed to our many responsibilities. Yet our spiritual growth is stunted and we cannot honestly describe our relationship with the Lord as intimate. The relationship is certainly deeper than casual, and clearly goes beyond being simply functional, but as the couple described in the example in Chapter Five it is not quite intimate. It is the busyness of ministry that can require the greatest level of balance in order to build a life of intimacy with God. We can deceive ourselves into thinking that the work we are doing in the church and for the church is satisfying the requirements of an intimate relationshlp. And yes, we must surely agree with the Word that we work because of our faith; that our work is the demonstration of our faith. However, we must also agree that as did Jesus, we must have that alone time with the Father to stay grounded and vibrant in doing the work. Otherwise we become like robots, doing things out of routine or obligation, not out of our passionate desire to please the Father.

Can any of us say that our schedules and demands are any greater than Jesus when He walked the earth? He was pulled in every direction imaginable. He couldn't even walk down the road to go help a dying girl without having someone crawl through the crowd and touch his clothes. He couldn't even go to a wedding without being asked to rescue the host who ran out of wine. He couldn't even try to get some "down time" at Peter's house without having to heal his mother-in-law or go to the temple to pray without having a withered hand on the agenda. Really. Jesus was always in demand on demand and yet He knew the value of getting alone to be with the Father. The way that He was able to confidently declare that He only did and spoke what His Father said is by being one with the Father. At one point He even said when you see me you see the Father (John 14:9), so clearly the level of intimacy the two of them shared was incomparable with any other. How many of us can scarcely whisper that we are one with the Father without focused fellowship with Him?

Simply said, we need to slow down, evaluate what we are doing, and determine if it is busy work, ministry or even public display for approval. Whatever the examination yields, we need to be ready to prioritize alone time in God's presence, listening for His voice, submitting to His will, and being willing to receive His filling afresh and anew. We need to pursue Him so fervently that He is able to say, like David, that we too are children after His own heart. That might mean letting some things go or at a minimum rearranging our priority and making it God. After all, being busy may not get you the "Well done thou good and faithful servant" response that we all long for. It just might get you that dreaded "Depart from me, I know you not" (Matthew 25), even after your list of achievements and accomplishments are recited in the Father's hearing. So slow down and get some much needed rest, resting that is, in the presence of the Lord. I promise you that you will see a spark of intimacy that both you and the Father long for.

Chapter Ten

WORLDLY DISTRACTIONS

Mark 4:18-20 "And these are they which are sown among thorns; such as hear the word, And the cares of this world, and the deceitfulness of riches, and the lusts of other things entering in, choke the word, and it becometh unfruitful." (KJV)

How can an intimate relationship with God compete with the myriad of distractions that exist and continue to emerge in this 21st Century? The truth of the matter is that any relationship trying to thrive in this era has to face some pretty major competition. I wish I could place the blame entirely on the times in which we live, but even in all the preceding centuries I am convinced that man has had some form of worldly distractions to undermine his relationships with both God and man. As deep and intimate a relationship as Solomon had with God he got so off track because of his worldly desires for women that he turned to serving other gods (I Kings 11:1-8). The apostles were even distracted in the first century by the murmuring and accusations of others, trying to provoke them to veer off course with good intentions when they were pressing toward full time ministry (Acts 6:1-4). Clearly it is nothing new that we, in an era where there is so much to stimulate the five senses, would be dazzled by what the world has to offer and become distracted. It is far easier to use the technology at hand to research the Bible, to hear sermons, to get inspirational messages, to even learn a new language. And exercising, walking or jogging in silence is definitely a thing of the past when you can have music pumped right into your ears. All of these things are a sign of progress, so why then would they even make it into this discussion?

Years ago when I first began falling in love with the Lord, I was so taken by my love for Him that I didn't really focus on the many distractions around me. I had already begun to make some decisions about a more godly lifestyle so many of the things the world did for fun were already leaving me. The computer was just emerging on the scene and I was excited just to give up correction tape and white out and yes, carbon paper. I was fascinated by the fact that I could edit or delete a word by the stroke of a key. In no time I was relying on those features, trying to imagine how my life was before. Of course the Internet was still a foreign land to me back then, but between the computer, the car phone that was in a bag in the car, the VHS and cassette tapes, I was a very happy camper. I played my tapes at night while I was sleeping and I watched wholesome videos and movies during my relaxation time. I plugged in the car phone in the car's lighter charger in an emergency. It couldn't get any better, or so I thought.

As the cell phone became more popular and my job required that I have one, I traded my phone in a bag for a big thick replica of today's cordless. I was making progress. Computers stopped reading 4 ½ floppy discs that got replaced by 3 ¼ and I lost some data. Television, laptops and video games began to dominate family life and I lost some family time. And so on. I think you get the picture. Before I knew it, I was texting, going on social media sites, taking pictures on my cell phone and emailing them, and enjoying the word of the day on some Christian website. I was still in love with the Lord, but the sweet times of sitting outside for hours basking in His presence, listening for a Word through nature or drinking in some awesome principle from the waves, had begun to slip away. I found myself falling right into the trappings of the day without noticing at first what was happening. Determined to hold some kind of a "relationship" standard, I was able to maintain my communion time in the mornings and at night, but even then I was often interrupted by the phone even if I chose not to answer it. That I was too accessible to the things that can distract me, no matter how important or relevant or convenient they might be, was becoming very clear. I soon came to realize that I was not content with the state I had fallen into and that I was going to have to be very deliberate in carving out my time with the Lord if I was going to maintain the intimacy with Him I desperately need. It is one of the times that the cliché of going back to the good ole days was a position of truth.

The scripture reference introducing this chapter seemed the best way to describe what was happening in my life, and as I looked around,

I knew I was not alone. As I surveyed the "fruit" of Christians in general, I recognized that we were not representing the Kingdom in the meaningful way I believe God intended in passages like Mark 16:16-20 declaring that signs and wonders shall follow us that believe and that we should go about in Jesus' power confirming His Word. Further Ephesians 3:20 reminds us that it is the power of God that works in us, so as I am often praying "Thy Kingdom come; Thy will be done in earth as it is in Heaven", I wonder if I have enough of His power working in me to be used for such Kingdom evidence. Too often I have sadly had to conclude that the "lusts of other things have made me unfruitful" (Mark 4:20). I had to come to terms with the fact that this kind of power only comes from a oneness with the Father and that oneness only comes from being in His presence, pursuing Him, being desperate for Him, doing only those things He says do. That was yet another "Aha" moment for me. It shook me; stirred me; forced me out of my state of complacency and brought me to this place of desiring more and more intimacy and oneness with God. My prayer for you is that you too, will have an "Aha' moment and let go of those distraction that may be robbing you of the uninterrupted sanctified time designated for just you and the Father, regardless to how important, relevant, progressive, essential, satisfying or fulfilling they may appear to be. No distraction is worthy to be compared to the priceless intimacy of being one with the Father.

Chapter Eleven

SELF DECEPTION

I John 1:8-10 "If we say that we have no sin, we deceive ourselves, and the truth is not in us. If we confess our sins, he is faithful and just to forgive us our sins, and to cleanse us from all unrighteousness. If we say that we have not sinned, we make him a liar, and his word is not in us." (KJV)

Possibly the scariest of all thieves is the one that I am calling self-deception. As I was in prayer one morning I was alerted by the Holy Spirit to pray because some people that I love that I am often concerned about where they are spiritually came to mind. I was specifically praying for the church but also for people in general to recognize that there is more to being in relationship with God than living the routinized lifestyles of convenience that we often embrace. The ugly realization that people simply do not know any better and that's why they don't do better created yet another of those "Aha" moments for me.

Let me begin this discussion with an online definition of self-deception that I found on Wikipedia.com. There were many dictionary sites, but this definition seemed to capture what I was thinking because it added the component of "convincing yourself". It defines self-deception as "a process of denying or rationalizing away the relevance, significance, or importance of opposing evidence and logical argument. Self-deception involves convincing oneself of a truth (or lack of truth) so that one does not reveal any self-knowledge of the deception".

As I considered Christianity, those of us who say we are Christians, I was grieved not only because of our lack of intimacy, but also because of the lack of power that accompanies it and worse our contentment with where we are. Those thoughts triggered the beginning of a journey for me and before I could put on the breaks I had traveled down an entire street of what that looks like. I thought about folk who do not go to church regularly, who choose to do most anything else they want to on the worship day except church, but quickly confess that they are Christians. Then folk who go to church and as a good deacon friend of mine who has long ago gone home to be with the Lord used to say, "punch their ticket" or in other words mark off on their list of things to do that they went to church, came to mind. Yet another group popped up and those are they who pray and possibly read some religious material occasionally, who can see for themselves and will often share with others how God has blessed, but they live like they want to without any true commitment to submit to the will of God. The street I was on kept getting longer and folk who do not believe they need to go to church at all but call themselves Christians because they can see God in nature and they live by good principles and they treat others as they would like to be treated showed up. Then there are the ones who call themselves Christians but do not believe that the whole Bible is true, just parts of it or who believe that it is just a book full of nice stories to give us examples to live by.

By the time I had experienced so many different kinds of illustrations of people who call themselves Christians, many who are in church, some who are not, but in some way representing that they are children of God, my heart was heavy. I imagined the joy the enemy was having because of his success in blinding the minds of those who do not believe (II Corinthians 4:4). I could not help but think how deceived we are; how ignorant we are to Satan's devices (II Corinthians 2:11) and how we have missed the most essential intimate relationship that could ever exist for us. There were people that I could think of who have said they stopped going to church for whatever reason but they follow the religious programs on television or the internet and that's enough for them. Or the people who go to church regularly and participate in ministries in the church but still do all the things that can be identified with the world, e. g. clubbing, partying, having sex outside of marriage, using illegal drugs, gambling, drinking, smoking, spending money they do not have, worrying, lying, gossiping, being unethical, and endorsing things that are contrary to godly principles (John the Baptist might call them hypocrites). The painful part of all this for me is that most people whose lifestyle reflects these symptoms are clueless that there is a problem. They are content with the life they live and find you quite arrogant, rude, sanctimonious and sometimes downright repulsive should you approach the subject with any form of correction or instruction. They have convinced themselves that they are fine; you are the extremist and that God is not nearly as rigid as you portray Him to be.

To give you a personal example of self-deception, I will share that many years ago I had an allergic reaction to something that made my lips break out. They were covered with a rash and were swollen and I had no idea what caused the problem. After medical attention did not reveal the cause, the dermatologist began to ask me questions about a history of allergy. I readily admitted no such history. He ran tests and prescribed ointments and nothing changed the condition. Again I was questioned about allergies and I knew I did not have any allergies. I suffered from sinusitis for sure, and certain prescription drugs gave me a headache and I had a horrible reaction to some sunscreen one summer, but allergies, no. The dermatologist decided to (just as a precaution) have me wear a large patch adhered to my back with a series of dots on it for a few days, asking me to be careful not to get it wet. I followed the instructions without deviation and returned to the office for the patch to be removed. When I was shown the patch, there were a few spots that were discolored so I immediately asked what that meant. The doctor said these are things that you are allergic to. Me? No way. I don't have allergies. People who suffer in the spring and can't take sulfur (like my sisters) or aspirin (like my girlfriend) or shellfish or you get the picture, those are the unfortunate folk who have allergies. Well it turned out that I have several skin allergies, one of which is to the content in the wax in Chap Stick, which I used regularly to keep my lips moistened. I have since discovered that the same ingredient was in the sunscreen that caused that summer reaction, and found out the hard way that it is also in many facial moisturizers. The good news is, once I acknowledged that I have allergies, I was able to live safer, healthier and wiser. I have no idea where the misconception that I did not have allergies came from, but it was real, demanding my best defense. I had convinced myself that what was true was not true for me and I was totally committed to my position. Thinking back on the visits to the dermatologist I can only be grateful that he was kind to me and extended me grace despite what he may have been thinking.

As I imagine how the Lord observes us in sadness, knowing that we have deceived ourselves into thinking that we are doing all right spiritually, that we are giving Him as much as we need to, that it really doesn't take "all that", my heart breaks. My heart's desire for us is that we really "know" the God who loves us and has made every provision for us to be one with Him. It cannot happen as long as we think we are doing fine, that He doesn't require even as much as we are giving Him, and that all those high standards He has set for us were expected to be adjusted to the times in which we live. I encourage us to examine our lifestyles, our motives, what motivates us, and even our false sense of arrogance as we consider moving toward a more intimate relationship with our great God.

Chapter Twelve

UNBELIEF

Hebrews 11:6 "But without faith it is impossible to please him: for he that cometh to God must believe that he is, and that he is a rewarder of them that diligently seek him." (KJV)

This chapter will be one of the briefest of all. There is just not a whole lot I can say if you do not believe that God is who He says He is. One may argue that unbelief can come in other forms that do not disbelieve who God is, but rather disbelieve that He will do what He says He will do at least when it pertains to you. I contend that those two things ultimately are the same. If we really believe who He is, we should have no problem believing every aspect of who He is. He cannot lie. He is all powerful. He is all knowing. He is everywhere present and ever-present. He is ever-loving. He is full of mercy. He is faithful. He is just. He is concerned about every detail of our lives. He is eternal. Of course these attributes are still but a tip of the iceberg of who God is, but because my limited thinking stopped right here, this is still quite enough to prove that He is worthy of your both believing in Him and believing Him, which are not the same.

What is unbelief? The Merriam-Webster online dictionary defines unbelief as "incredulity or skepticism especially in matters of religious faith". Synonyms for incredulity are suspicion, doubt, disbelief. Skepticism which may be a bit more familiar to us has synonyms like uncertainty, distrust and cynicism. All of these words point in the same direction. There is insufficient faith in someone to accept who they are unconditionally without questioning. And I say "someone" deliberately because I don't believe you can believe or have faith in "something". I believe that belief is relational. Objects or concepts really only provoke you to accept the fact(s) about that thing. Belief/faith extends far beyond facts and that is the only way we can accept who God is. Simple faith; no wavering, no looking for motives, no examining His capabilities, just receiving Him for who He is, which is often in defiance of the facts, is the only way to believe that He is. So if you cannot believe that He is, you cannot please Him. If you cannot please Him, you cannot be in relationship with Him. If you cannot be in relationship with Him, there is no chance for intimacy. End of story.

CONCLUSION

As you have come to the end of this journey with me, my prayer for you is found in Ephesians 3:14-21.

> "For this cause I bow my knees unto the Father of our Lord Jesus Christ, [15] Of whom the whole family in heaven and earth is named, [16] That he would grant you, according to the riches of his glory, to be strengthened with might by his Spirit in the inner man; [17] That Christ may dwell in your hearts by faith; that ye, being rooted and grounded in love, [18] May be able to comprehend with all saints what is the breadth, and length, and depth, and height; [19] And to know the love of Christ, which passeth knowledge, that ye might be filled with all the fulness of God. [20] Now unto him that is able to do exceeding abundantly above all that we ask or think, according to the power that worketh in us, [21] Unto him be glory in the church by Christ Jesus throughout all ages, world without end. Amen." (KJV)

CPSIA information can be obtained at www.ICGtesting.com
Printed in the USA
BVOW05s1151030215

386169BV00001B/3/P